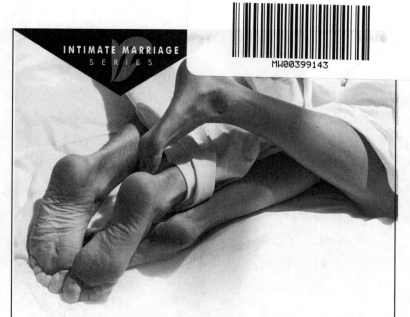

SEXUAL INTIMACY

Dan B. Allender
and Tremper Longman III

6 STUDIES FOR INDIVIDUALS, COUPLES OR GROUPS

InterVarsity Press
Downers Grove, Illinois

InterVarsity Press
P.O. Box 1400, Downers Grove, IL 60515-1426
World Wide Web: www.ivpress.com
E-mail: mail@ivpress.com

InterVarsity Press® is the book-publishing division of InterVarsity Christian Fellowship/USA®, a student movement active on campus at hundreds of universities, colleges and schools of nursing in the United States of America, and a member movement of the International Fellowship of Evangelical Students. For information about local and regional activities, write Public Relations Dept., InterVarsity Christian Fellowship/USA, 6400 Schroeder Rd., P.O. Box 7895, Madison, WI 53707-7895, or visit the IVCF website at <www.intervarsity.org>.

Design: Cindy Kiple

Images: Regine Mahaux/Getty Images

ISBN 0-8308-2137-6

Printed in the United States of America ∞

P	18	17	16	15	14	13	12	11	10	9	8	7	6	5	4	3	2	1
Y	18	17	16	15	14	13	12	11	10	09	08	07	06	05				

CONTENTS

Welcome to Intimate Marriage Bible Studies. 5

1 DESIRE AND ECSTASY 9
Song of Songs 6:13—7:13

2 DIFFERENT BODIES 15
Song of Songs 4:1—5:1, 10-16

3 TIME FOR PASSION 22
Song of Songs 1:2-4, 7-17

4 OVERCOMING CONTEMPT AND SHAME 28
Genesis 2:25—3:17; 2 Samuel 6:14-16, 20-22

5 RESTORING BROKEN TRUST 35
Psalm 55

6 LOVE'S FAILURE AND REDEMPTION 40
Song of Songs 5:2—6:3

Leader's Notes 47

WELCOME TO
INTIMATE MARRIAGE
BIBLE STUDIES

SEXUAL INTIMACY

Nothing brings more joy and more trouble to a marriage relationship than sex. When things click, other problems seem manageable, but when connection is difficult or nonexistent the whole world turns bleak.

Often young people fantasize about marriage as a time of complete sexual fulfillment. After all, with a spouse, sex is possible anytime and anyplace. But the reality is that the potential for misconnection is high. Sometimes one's spouse is out of the mood or angry and doesn't want to be intimate. At other times, they may be sick and can't enjoy it. And often time and energy are in short supply. After a particularly busy day with work and children, a husband and/or a wife find it difficult to romp in the bedroom.

Christians are often confused about sexuality, and the church doesn't offer much help. Most of the Bible guards against promiscuous sex outside of the commitment of marriage, and the church trumpets that message. However, the Bible also teaches about the pleasures of God's good gift of sexuality, and the following studies direct our attention to those passages while also presenting a realistic picture of the difficulties of connection in a fallen world.

TAKING MARRIAGE SERIOUSLY

Most of us want to have a good marriage. Those who don't have a good relationship yearn for a better one, and those who have a good one want even more intimacy.

We want to know our spouse and be known by them. We want to be loved and to love. In short, we want the type of marriage desired by God from the beginning when he created the institution of marriage and defined it as involving leaving parents, weaving a life of intimacy together and cleaving in sexual bliss.

These studies delve into the wisdom of the Bible in order to learn what it takes to have not just a "good" marriage but one that enjoys the relational richness that God intended for a husband and a wife. This divinely instituted type of marriage is one that will

- Bring a husband and wife closer together
- Understand that marriage is one's primary loyalty to other human beings
- Be characterized by a growing love and knowledge of one another
- Be an arena of spiritual growth
- Allow for the healthy exposure of sin through the offer of forgiveness
- Be a crucible for showing grace
- Reflect God's love for his people
- Enjoy God's gift of sexual intimacy
- Share life's joys and troubles
- Have a part in transforming us from sinners to saints

- Bring out each other's glory as divine image bearers

And so much more! The Bible provides a wealth of insight, and these studies hope to tap its riches and bring them to bear on our marriage relationships.

USING THE STUDIES

These studies can be used in a variety of contexts—individual devotional life, by a couple together or by a small group—or in a combination of these settings. Each study includes the following components.

Open. Several quotes at the beginning give a sense of what married people say about the topic at hand. These are followed by a question that can be used for discussion. If you are using the DVD, you may want to skip this and go straight to the opening clip.

DVD Reflection. For each session we have an opening thought from Dan Allender, at times accompanied by an excerpt from our interviews with married couples, to get you thinking about the topic at hand. This material will provide fresh and engaging openers for a small group as well as interesting discussion points for couples studying together. You will find a question here to discuss after you watch the DVD clip.

Study. One or more key Bible texts are included in the guide for convenience. We have chosen the New Living Translation, but you may use any version of Scripture you like. The questions in this section will take you through the key aspects of the passage and help you apply them to your marriage. Sprinkled throughout the study, you will also find commentary to enrich your experience.

For the Couple. Here's an opportunity to make an application and commitment, which is specific to your marriage.

Bonus. These are further ideas for study on your own. Or if you are studying with a group, take time to do the bonus item with your spouse during the week.

We hope that these studies enrich your marriage. We encourage you to be brutally honest with yourself and tactfully honest with your spouse. If you are willing to be honest with yourself and with the Scripture, then God will do great things for your marriage. That is our prayer.

DESIRE AND ECSTASY

"Is it wrong to want intimacy?"

"The Bible teaches that sex is for having babies."

"Sex is dirty, and I am embarrassed to talk about it, even with my wife."

"Sex is the most beautiful thing in the world."

▶ OPEN

God created human beings with a strong desire for sexual touch. Our bodies are wired in such a way as to respond with pleasure, even ecstasy, when stroked in special ways. Why then do God's people feel so conflicted about sex?

▶ DVD REFLECTION

How has your faith shaped your views on sexuality?

▶ STUDY

Song of Songs helps us understand how Christians should view sexual relationships both in marriage and outside of it. We are not sure who the man and the woman in the Song of Solomon are, but they stand for every married couple. A couple reading the Song is to put themselves in the place of the young man and the young woman. The Song encourages us toward romance and helps us develop a language of love.

Read Song of Songs 6:13—7:13.

Young Women of Jerusalem

¹³Return, return to us, O maid of
    Shulam.
   Come back, come back, that we
    may see you again.

Young Man

Why do you stare at this young
    woman of Shulam,
   as she moves so gracefully be-
    tween two lines of dancers?

7 How beautiful are your
    sandaled feet, O queenly
    maiden.
Your rounded thighs are like jewels,
    the work of a skilled craftsman.
²Your navel is perfectly formed
   like a goblet filled with mixed
    wine.
Between your thighs lies a mound
    of wheat
   bordered with lilies.
³Your breasts are like two fawns,

twin fawns of a gazelle.
⁴Your neck is as beautiful as an
    ivory tower.
Your eyes are like the sparkling
    pools in Heshbon
   by the gate of Bath-rabbim.
Your nose is as fine as the tower
    of Lebanon
   overlooking Damascus.
⁵Your head is as majestic as
    Mount Carmel,
   and the sheen of your hair
    radiates royalty.
   The king is held captive by its
    tresses.
⁶Oh, how beautiful you are!
   How pleasing, my love, how full
    of delights!
⁷You are slender like a palm tree,
   and your breasts are like its
    clusters of fruit.
⁸I said, "I will climb the palm tree
   and take hold of its fruit."
May your breasts be like

grape clusters,
and the fragrance of your breath
like apples.
[9]May your kisses be as exciting as
the best wine,
flowing gently over lips and
teeth.

Young Woman

[10]I am my lover's,
and he claims me as his own.
[11]Come, my love, let us go out to
the fields
and spend the night among the
wildflowers.

[12]Let us get up early and go to the
vineyards
to see if the grapevines have
budded,
if the blossoms have opened,
and if the pomegranates have
bloomed.
There I will give you my love.
[13]There the mandrakes give off their
fragrance,
and the finest fruits are at our
door,
new delights as well as old,
which I have saved for you,
my lover.

READING METAPHORS

Metaphors reverberate through the Song of Songs, particularly in descriptions of the physical beauty of the man and the woman. Metaphors bring together two things that are essentially dissimilar except in one striking way. To interpret a metaphor, the reader must reflect on that similarity. For instance, in what way is the man's beloved like a palm tree with clusters of dates? She may be tall and slim, but it is clear from this metaphor that the object of his romantic and sensuous attention is her breasts, which are like date clusters on a palm.

1. From these verses, how would you describe the man's feelings
toward the woman?

WATCHING HER DANCE

The dance referred to in verse 6:13 is probably being compared to a clash between two armies. To watch the woman dance is like watching two armies in battle: mesmerizing.

Imagine yourself on a hill looking down into a valley where two armies are meeting in battle. You can't take your eyes off the spectacle. The same is true as the man watches his beloved dance. It thrills him and makes his knees knock. This verse is one of a number of places in the Song where the poet uses military language to describe the thrill and awe that a man feels in the presence of his beloved.

2. Do you think this type of passionate expression is necessary to a marriage? Why or why not?

   How do you relate to this sense of passion from your own experience?

3. Why do the lovers want to go to the countryside to share their intimacies (7:11)?

4. Explore the man's description of the woman's body. Select several of the images he presents and ask what they signify.

5. What is the woman's response to the man's speech (7:10-13)?

6. How might the man and woman's relationship be strengthened by this kind of frank and detailed conversation?

7. As you reflect on the meaning of the woman's name, Shulammite (see the sidebar on the next page), what does that tell you about the goal of this intimate relationship?

▼

THE SHULAMMITE

When for the first time in the book the woman is given a name of sorts, she is called the Shulammite (6:13, in the NLT the "maid of Shulam"). There is much debate about the significance of this name, but a couple of observations may be made. In the first place, this is the feminine equivalent to Solomon, whose name in Hebrew is Sholomo. Second, both names are formed from the common Hebrew word shalom, which means peace or contentment. So these are the songs of Solomon, and the recipient is the Shulammite; their intimate relationship brings satisfaction, contentment and peace.

▶ FOR THE COUPLE

As we have seen, the name of the woman in Song of Songs means "contentment"; probably this is a statement about the consequences of her relationship with the man. In what ways does your relationship bring you contentment?

How can your relationship grow toward greater contentment?

▶ BONUS

In the Sermon on the Mount, Jesus warns against the dangers of lusting after a woman. His warning goes so far as to suggest gouging out one's eyes if they cause one to lust. Does that mean we can't feel any sense of arousal toward our beloved until we are married? Why or why not?

2

DIFFERENT BODIES

"The Bible teaches that looks are unimportant. You should marry a woman based only on her love of God and her character. Beauty is only skin deep."

"Ever since my husband has put on so much weight, I find it hard to be aroused by him."

▶ OPEN

Men and women are made differently. While this statement covers more than anatomy, it certainly includes physical appearance. What is it about a woman that attracts a man and vice versa?

▶ DVD REFLECTION

What differences have you noticed between how each of you offers and receives love?

▶ STUDY

Read Song of Songs 4:1—5:1, 10-16.

Young Man

4　You are beautiful, my darling,
　　beautiful beyond words.
Your eyes are like doves
　　behind your veil.
Your hair falls in waves,
　　like a flock of goats winding
　　　down the slopes of Gilead.
[2]Your teeth are as white as sheep,
　　recently shorn and freshly
　　　washed.
Your smile is flawless,
　　each tooth matched with its
　　　twin.
[3]Your lips are like scarlet ribbon;
　　your mouth is inviting.
Your cheeks are like rosy
　　　pomegranates
　　behind your veil.
[4]Your neck is as beautiful as the
　　　tower of David,
　　jeweled with the shields of a
　　　thousand heroes.
[5]Your breasts are like two fawns,
　　twin fawns of a gazelle grazing
　　　among the lilies.
[6]Before the dawn breezes blow
　　and the night shadows flee,
I will hurry to the mountain of
　　　myrrh
　　and to the hill of frankincense.
[7]You are altogether beautiful,
　　my darling,
　　beautiful in every way.

[8]Come with me from Lebanon,
　　my bride,
　　come with me from Lebanon.
Come down from Mount Amana,
　　from the peaks of Senir and
　　　Hermon,
where lions have their dens
　　and leopards live among the hills.

[9]You have captured my heart,
　　my treasure, my bride.
You hold it hostage with one glance
　　of your eyes,
　　with a single jewel of your
　　　necklace.
[10]Your love delights me,
　　my treasure, my bride.
Your love is better than wine,
　　your perfume more fragrant
　　　than spices.
[11]Your lips are as sweet as nectar, my
　　　bride.
　　Honey and milk are under your
　　　tongue.
Your clothes are scented
　　like the cedars of Lebanon.

[12]You are my private garden,
　　my treasure, my bride,
　　a secluded spring, a hidden
　　　fountain.

[13]Your thighs shelter a paradise of
  pomegranates
with rare spices—
henna with nard
[14] nard and saffron,
  fragrant calamus and cinnamon,
with all the trees of frankincense,
  myrrh, and aloes,
  and every other lovely spice.
[15]You are a garden fountain,
  a well of fresh water
  streaming down from Lebanon's
  mountains.

Young Woman

[16]Awake, north wind!
  Rise up, south wind!
Blow on my garden
  and spread its fragrance all
  around.
Come into your garden, my love;
  taste its finest fruits.

Young Man

5 I have entered my garden, my
  treasure, my bride!
  I gather myrrh with my spices
and eat honeycomb with my honey.
  I drink my wine with my milk.

Young Women of Jerusalem

Oh, lover and beloved, eat and
  drink!
  Yes, drink deeply of your love!

Young Woman

[10]My lover is dark and dazzling,
  better than ten thousand others!
[11]His head is finest gold,
  his wavy hair is black as a raven.
[12]His eyes sparkle like doves
  beside springs of water;
they are set like jewels
  washed in milk.
[13]His cheeks are like gardens of
  spices
  giving off fragrance.
His lips are like lilies,
  perfumed with myrrh.
[14]His arms are like rounded bars of
  gold,
  set with beryl.
His body is like bright ivory,
  glowing with lapis lazuli.
[15]His legs are like marble pillars
  set in sockets of finest gold.
His posture is stately,
  like the noble cedars of Lebanon.
[16]His mouth is sweetness itself;
  he is desirable in every way.
Such, O women of Jerusalem,
  is my lover, my friend.

1. These poems exult in the physical beauty of the woman and the man. But what if you don't feel beautiful?

What if you don't even believe that your spouse is beautiful?

2. Proverbs 31:30 says, "Charm is deceptive, and beauty does not last; / but a woman who fears the LORD will be greatly praised." Does this teaching contradict the emphasis on physical beauty in these two poems in the Song? Explain your response.

3. Note how the man and the woman praise each other by drawing analogies (using metaphors). Her eyes are like doves, her lips like a scarlet ribbon and so on. His cheeks are beds of spices, his legs like pillars of marble. What do these metaphors mean?

GARDENS IN THE SONG OF SONGS

Throughout the Song of Songs we encounter garden imagery. Some-times the garden is the place where the man and the woman meet to enjoy intimate moments, and sometimes the garden is descriptive of the woman's body (as in 4:12-15). In the light of other ancient Near Eastern love poems, we know that the garden metaphor is a discreet way of referring to the most private and sensual place in the woman's body, the object of lovemaking. That this is the case here is underlined by the use of another well-known metaphor, the fountain (see also Proverbs 5:15-20).

4. The poem that describes the woman's beauty concludes by praising the fragrance of her garden. Finally the woman invites the man into her garden, where he says, "I gather myrrh with my spices / and eat honeycomb with my honey. / I drink wine with my milk." What does this climactic moment in the poem signify?

5. Read through the poem and note the different references to the excitement of the senses as the man and the woman describe each other's body. How does this help a married couple learn how to enjoy each other?

WHY IS SUCH AN EROTIC BOOK
IN THE HOLY BIBLE?

The descriptive poems of the Song of Songs (4:1—5:1, 10-16; 6:4-9; 7:1-9) are among the most sensual parts of this most sensual of all biblical books. The poet waxes eloquent about the woman's fawnlike breasts, wine-filled navel and jewel-like inner thighs, as well as the man's ivory-hard body and pillarlike legs.

Many are shocked that such intimate descriptions are found in the Bible. What does the body have to do with the spirit? Apparently a lot! God created us whole beings and is concerned about us body and soul. The Song of Songs is a celebration of marital sexuality and encourages God's people to enjoy God's gift of sexuality.

6. Much of the language is quite erotic, referring to the woman's breasts, for instance. Is such language appropriate? In what situations?

7. In 4:8-9 the man invites the woman to come down from the dangerous mountain area where wild animals might harm her. It is unlikely that the poem is to be taken literally, as if she actually lived near wild animals. What do you think the poet is trying to communicate at this point?

▶ FOR THE COUPLE

Take time to write a short descriptive poem for your spouse. Use your own language to compliment his or her attractiveness. If poetry is difficult or awkward for you, simply write a love letter.

▶ BONUS

Read 1 Peter 3:3-6. Talk about what makes a woman truly beautiful and desirable. Does this conflict with the Song of Songs?

3

TIME FOR PASSION

"Our life is just too busy. If we are lucky enough to find time for sex, it isn't very much time. There is not much 'fore' to our play."

"The more time we spend building up to the moment, the more pleasurable it is."

▶ OPEN

In this busy world, our love life can disappear in a flood of commitments, work and just plain exhaustion. Married couples struggle to find time for each other. Even sex can become a quick routine that serves to relieve tension for the moment. But routine can soon become boring, and sex becomes more a duty than a joy. What strategies have you been able to employ to make time in your lives for sex?

▶ DVD REFLECTION

What keeps couples from finding time to be together?

▶ STUDY

The Song of Songs invites and encourages a sexual playfulness that can rekindle the spark of romance in a marriage.

Read Song of Songs 1:2-4, 7-17.

Young Woman

[2]Kiss me and kiss me again,
   for your love is sweeter than
      wine.
[3]How fragrant your cologne;
   your name is like its spreading
      fragrance.
   No wonder all the young
      women love you!
[4]Take me with you; come, let's run!
   The king has brought me into his
      bedroom.

Young Women of Jerusalem

How happy we are for you, O king,
   We praise your love even
      more than wine.

Young Woman

[7]Tell me, my love, where are you
      leading your flock today?
   Where will you rest your sheep
      at noon?
For why should I wander like a
   prostitute

among your friends and their
   flocks?

Young Man

[8]If you don't know, O most beautiful
      woman,
   follow the trail of my flock,
   and graze your young goats by
      the shepherds' tents.
[9]You are as exciting, my darling,
   as a mare among Pharaoh's
      stallions.
[10]How lovely are your cheeks;
   your earrings set them afire!
How lovely is your neck,
   enhanced by a string of jewels.
[11]We will make for you earrings of
      gold
   and beads of silver.

Young Woman

[12]The king is lying on his couch,
   enchanted by the fragrance of
      my perfume.
[13]My lover is like a sachet of myrrh

lying between my breasts.
[14]He is like a bouquet of sweet henna
   blossoms
from the vineyards of En-gedi.

Young Man

[15]How beautiful you are, my darling,
   how beautiful!
Your eyes are like doves.

Young Woman

[16]You are so handsome, my love,
   pleasing beyond words!
The soft grass is our bed;
   [17]fragrant cedar branches are the
   beams of our house,
and pleasant smelling firs are
   the rafters.

▼

KING AND SHEPHERD

In this chapter the woman refers to the man as both a king and a shepherd. Many people have erroneously assumed that the Song tells a story about a king and thus that the shepherd is a second character. These poems celebrate love through the use of sensuous imagery. In the eyes of the woman, her husband is a king. She also imagines him as a shepherd, creating a romantic pastoral setting for her musings about their love. As couples read these poems, the wife is to think of her husband as the king-shepherd, and the husband is to consider his wife to be the woman who speaks and acts in these poems.

1. As the woman describes how wonderful the man is, which sensual pleasures does she mention?

What does this imply for our own desires?

2. How is the man's love like, and even better than, wine?

3. In verse 3 the woman praises the man's name or reputation. What is it about reputation that intensifies attraction or repels?

NAME AND REPUTATION

In the Old Testament name means "reputation." To praise his name means that the woman gives honor to him and perhaps even brags about him to others.

4. The woman pursues the man in this poem, inviting him to bring her into his bedroom. In other words, she initiates foreplay. Do you think it is appropriate for a woman to take the lead in a relationship? Why or why not?

If not, then how do you understand this passage?

5. In this passage, a chorus of young women chimes in to voice approval of the relationship. Who are these women?

6. Why doesn't the man give her a direct answer (v. 8) when she asks where she can find him (v. 7)?

WHAT'S GOING ON?

The passage begins with a teasing interchange between the woman and the man, who is here described as a shepherd. She wants to be with him and suggests a meeting during his lunch rest. As a shepherd he would be away from people and their meeting in the countryside would provide an intimate setting. She asks him to tell her where he will be so she doesn't have to go tent-to-tent looking for him. If she does have to go tent-to-tent, the men might get the wrong impression of her and think that she is one of those girls who goes out to the tents of shepherds to offer her sexual favors.

7. The woman wears jewels to enhance her beauty (vv. 10-11). Do you think this is appropriate? Why or why not?

▶ FOR THE COUPLE

Do you care about your own looks? How about how your spouse looks? Why or why not?

What can or should you do to enhance the beauty of your spouse?

Share with each other what arouses you to desire sexual intimacy. Try not to get defensive, since often men and women move toward passion in different ways.

▶ BONUS

Read Ecclesiastes 3:1, 5. This poem suggests that God has created the proper time for all things. Verse 5 applies this to sexual embrace. How does one determine when it is the right time?

SCATTERING AND GATHERING STONES

Ecclesiastes 3:1-8 is a moving poem about God creating the right time for all things. It does so by citing opposites. These usually come in pairs of opposites, so verse 2 pairs a time to be born and a time to die with a time to plant and a time to harvest, the latter being the birth and death of a plant.

This observation may help us understand the significance of scattering and gathering stones, which is paired with embracing and turning away. The early Jewish Midrash offers a connection when it says: "A time to cast stones—when your wife is clean (menstrually), and a time to gather stones in—when your wife is unclean." The point that rabbis are making is that people should realize that there is a right time for a married couple to make love and a wrong time.

4

OVERCOMING CONTEMPT AND SHAME

"I can't stand my body. It disgusts me. How can I act sexy with my husband if I don't feel the least bit attractive?"

"Every time we have sex, I think about all my other girlfriends before we were married and before I was a Christian. Now sex just seems dirty, even though I'm married to her."

"I can't get aroused without fantasizing about somebody else. She just doesn't look as sensual as the girls in magazines."

"I hate being vulnerable, physically or emotionally. I don't want to get hurt again."

▶ OPEN

All marriage relationships struggle with obstacles to intimacy. What are some of the obstacles people face?

▶ DVD REFLECTION

What false expectations about sexuality have you noticed on television and in the movies?

▶ STUDY

In this study we come to understand some of these obstacles by looking at the wisdom of several Scripture passages.

Read Genesis 2:25—3:17.

²⁵Now the man and his wife were both naked, but they felt no shame.

3 The serpent was the shrewdest of all the wild animals the LORD God had made. One day he asked the woman, "Did God really say you must not eat the fruit from any of the trees in the garden?"

²"Of course we may eat fruit from the trees in the garden," the woman replied. ³"It's only the fruit from the tree in the middle of the garden that we are not allowed to eat. God said, 'You must not eat it or even touch it; if you do, you will die.' "

⁴"You won't die!" the serpent replied to the woman. ⁵"God knows that your eyes will be opened as soon as you eat it, and you will be like God, knowing both good and evil."

⁶The woman was convinced. She saw that the tree was beautiful and its fruit looked delicious, and she wanted the wisdom it would give her. So she took some of the fruit and ate it. Then she gave some to her husband, who was with her, and he ate it, too. ⁷At that moment their eyes were opened, and they suddenly felt shame at their nakedness. So they sewed fig leaves together to cover themselves.

⁸When the cool evening breezes were blowing, the man and his wife heard the LORD God walking about in the garden. So they hid from the LORD God among the trees.⁹ Then the LORD God called to the man, "Where are you?"

¹⁰He replied, "I heard you walking in the garden, so I hid. I was afraid because I was naked."

¹¹"Who told you that you were naked?" the LORD God asked. "Have you eaten from the tree whose fruit I commanded you not to eat?"

¹²The man replied, "It was the woman you gave me who gave me the fruit, and I ate it."

¹³Then the LORD God asked the woman, "What have you done?"

"The serpent deceived me," she replied. "That's why I ate it."

¹⁴Then the LORD God said to the serpent,

"Because you have done this, you are cursed
    more than all animals, domestic and wild.
You will crawl on your belly,
    groveling in the dust as long as you live.
¹⁵And I will cause hostility between you and the woman,
    and between your offspring and her offspring.
He will strike your head,
    and you will strike his heel."

¹⁶Then he said to the woman,

"I will sharpen the pain of your pregnancy,
    and in pain you will give birth.
And you will desire to control your husband,
    but he will rule over you."

¹⁷And to the man he said,

"Since you listened to your wife and ate from the tree
    whose fruit I commanded you not to eat,
the ground is cursed because of you.
    All your life you will struggle to scratch a living from it."

1. Does the story of the Fall ring true to you? Why or why not?

2. How do husbands and wives try to dominate each other?

EVE'S DESIRE

The significance of Eve's desire can be easily misunderstood in this context. One reading would take "desire" in a positive sense, that is, Eve has romantic desire to be in an intimate relationship with her husband. The curse then is that Adam responds by control and domination.

The Hebrew word translated "desire" in Genesis 3:16 occurs only two other times in the Bible. The one that is relevant to our understanding here is in Genesis 4:7, where it describes sin's desire for Cain. Eve's desire in Genesis 3:16, then, is not a romantic longing but a desire to dominate Adam. The couple enters a power struggle, which the man will usually win.

Why do husbands and wives try to dominate each other?

3. How do relational power struggles affect intimacy?

4. What is the solution to the problem?

Read 2 Samuel 6:14-16, 20-22.

[14]And David danced before the LORD with all his might, wearing a priestly garment. [15]So David and all the people of Israel brought up the Ark of the LORD with shouts of joy and the blowing of rams' horns.

[16]But as the Ark of the LORD entered the City of David, Michal, the daughter of Saul, looked down from her window. When she saw King David leaping and dancing before the LORD, she was filled with contempt for him.

[20]When David returned home to bless his own family, Michal, the daughter of Saul, came out to meet him. She said in disgust, "How distinguished the king of Israel looked today, shamelessly exposing himself to the servant girls like any vulgar person might do!"

[21]David retorted to Michal, "I was dancing before the LORD, who chose me above your father and all his family! He appointed me as the leader of Israel, the people of the LORD, so I celebrate before the LORD. [22]Yes, and I am willing to look even more foolish than this, even to be humiliated in my own eyes! But those servant girls you mentioned will indeed think I am distinguished!"

5. Describe Michal's reaction to David's dancing. Does she have a reason to feel upset?

6. How about David? Does he respond well to Michal's criticism? Explain.

THE ARK OF THE COVENANT

Described in Exodus 25:10-22, the ark was constructed from a rather simple design. It was a relatively small box, 3¾ feet long, 2¼ feet wide and 2¼ feet high. Rings were attached to the sides, through which poles were slid for carrying it. Made of precious acacia wood, the ark was covered inside and out by the finest gold.

But what is truly important is this box's significance. It was the most potent symbol of the presence of God for Israelites throughout the Old Testament period. Indeed, it was seen as the footstool of God's throne (1 Chronicles 28:2), perhaps even occasionally as the throne itself (Jeremiah 3:16-17).

The moment recorded in 2 Samuel 6 is fraught with significance. King David had recently captured Jerusalem from the Jebusites and made it his capital. The ark, taken by the Philistines earlier and then returned, had been lodged in a small town called Kiriath-jearim until this moment. Now the ark is coming to David's new capital, and he reacts with great joy.

7. This text is not in the Bible primarily to teach us about the institution of marriage; it is addressing other important political and theological issues. However, Michal's reaction to David reflects a dynamic often seen in marriage. Setting aside the text's theological and political concerns, put yourself in Michal's place. Michal has just seen her husband do something that shamed her. How should she react?

Now take David's point of view. How should he react?

8. How does this text illuminate the corrosive effects of anger and contempt on a relationship?

▶ FOR THE COUPLE

Think back to a time when one of you felt shamed by the other's words or behavior. Were you able to talk about it?

If any aspect of that event or the discussion of it has remained unresolved, be honest with each other about that—prayerfully. Make any needed explanations and apologies, and offer forgiveness.

Is there a symbolic way you can now honor each other, to move further toward reconciliation?

▶ BONUS

When we think of our weaknesses, we often experience the contempt of others, and shame wells up inside ourselves. What does 2 Corinthians 12:9-10 say about our weaknesses?

Should our weaknesses debilitate us? Why or why not?

RESTORING
BROKEN TRUST

"I've put my husband through a lot. How can I make it up to him?"

"I've been hurt so many times when I opened myself up to another. No way am I going to allow myself to get really close to someone."

"My wife has turned down my advances so often that I have just about given up. I'm afraid to approach her sexually because I take the rejection so hard."

▶ OPEN

Fear alienates. It drives us to seek shelter from others so we can't get hurt. In a sense it is the opposite of anger. When we feel assaulted, either we lash back to drive someone away or we shrink back for fear of hurt.

If fear separates people, then it is obvious that it works against intimacy. Fear is an enemy of marriage. What can we do about our fears?

▶ DVD REFLECTION

What does it take to be safe and trustworthy to each other in a marriage?

▶ STUDY

Psalm 55 is identified in the title as a psalm of David, so its content certainly flowed out of a situation in his life. However, the psalms, though inspired by specific events in the composer's life, are written in such a way as to be applicable to similar situations in other people's lives. David wrote this psalm not so that we would remember his struggle with fear but so other people might have a prayer to apply to their own situation.

Read Psalm 55.

For the choir director: A psalm of David, to be accompanied by stringed instruments.

¹Listen to my prayer, O God.
 Do not ignore my cry for help!
²Please listen and answer me,
 for I am overwhelmed by my
  troubles.
³My enemies shout at me,
 making loud and wicked
  threats.
They bring trouble on me
 and angrily hunt me down.

⁴My heart pounds in my chest.
 The terror of death assaults me.
⁵Fear and trembling overwhelm me,
 and I can't stop shaking.
⁶Oh, that I had wings like a dove;
 then I would fly away and rest!
⁷I would fly far away

to the quiet of the wilderness.
⁸How quickly I would escape—
 far from this wild storm of hatred.

⁹Confuse them, Lord, and frustrate
  their plans,
 for I see violence and conflict in
  the city.
¹⁰Its walls are patrolled day and night
  against invaders,
 but the real danger is
  wickedness within the city.
¹¹Everything is falling apart;
 threats and cheating are
  rampant in the streets.

¹²It is not an enemy who taunts me—
 I could bear that.
It is not my foes who so arrogantly
  insult me—
 I could have hidden from them.

[13]Instead, it is you—my equal,
  my companion and close friend.
[14]What good fellowship we once
    enjoyed
    as we walked together to the
    house of God.

[15]Let death stalk my enemies;
  let the grave swallow them alive,
  for evil makes its home within
    them.

[16]But I will call on God,
  and the LORD will rescue me.
[17]Morning, noon, and night
  I cry out in my distress,
  and the LORD hears my voice.
[18]He ransoms me and keeps me safe
  from the battle waged against me,
  though many still oppose me.
[19]God, who has ruled forever,
  will hear me and humble them.

For my enemies refuse to change
    their ways;
    they do not fear God.

[20]As for my companion, he betrayed
    his friends;
    he broke his promises.
[21]His words are as smooth as butter,
  but in his heart is war.
His words are as soothing as lotion,
  but underneath are daggers!

[22]Give your burdens to the LORD,
  and he will take care of you.
  He will not permit the godly to
    slip and fall.
[23]But you, O God, will send the
    wicked
  down to the pit of destruction.
Murderers and liars will die young,
  but I am trusting you to save me.

1. In verse 5, the psalmist says that "fear and trembling over-whelm" him. What does the psalm say is frightening him?

2. Note who the psalmist feels most threatened by. What is particularly tough about the situation?

3. The psalmist is clearly shaken by the attack of his friend. How does the psalmist react?

4. When you feel attacked by a friend or someone more intimate like your spouse, how do you react?

DEGREES OF FEAR

Psalm 55 expresses an extreme level of fear that leads the psalmist to want to flee the city and also motivates him to ask the Lord to remove the offending party. However, such utter terror is related to less extreme forms, including anxiety. What we learn about fear from the psalm is true, though perhaps to a lesser extent, about worry and anxiety.

5. What is it about a loved one's betrayal that is especially unsettling?

What past experience of betrayal have you had?

6. What happens to a close relationship like marriage when one loses trust because of an attack? (Consider the psalmist's words in verses 6-7.)

7. How can a marriage preserve vulnerability but avoid fear?

8. If one or both spouses in a marriage feel anxious or fearful in the relationship, what can they do?

▶ FOR THE COUPLE

Individually, think about those areas in your relationship where you are afraid to expose yourself to your spouse. Ask why you feel this fear. If possible, talk about this with your spouse.

▶ BONUS

Read Judges 16:4-22. While fear in a good marriage is counterproductive, is there ever a time when fear can serve a constructive purpose?

6

LOVE'S FAILURE
AND REDEMPTION

"All my husband cares about is sex. I get up in the morning and he is all over me. If he were only more romantic, I would probably enjoy it more."

"My husband pays no attention to me whatsoever. He gets up in the morning and goes to work, and when he gets home, he just gets a drink and sits in front of the television like a zombie. Our sex life is at a virtual zero."

"My wife and I only rarely get on the same page when it comes to sex. When I want to have sex, she's too tired. When she does, I have to get to work. It seems such a hassle."

"Though it is a struggle, when we do have sex, it is sublime."

▶ OPEN

People who have been married for a while will attest that at some time in their relationship they felt completely out of sync sexually. What are the things that keep us from enjoying one another sexually?

▶ DVD REFLECTION

What does God have to do with sexuality in a marriage?

▶ STUDY

The Song of Songs, though passionate in its celebration of love, is still a realistic book. It recognizes that married couples do encounter obstacles to union. But it also points the way to the remedy.

Read Song of Songs 5:2—6:3.

Young Woman

[2]I slept, but my heart was awake,
   when I heard my lover knocking
      and calling:
"Open to me, my treasure, my
      darling,
   my dove, my perfect one.
My head is drenched with dew,
   my hair with the dampness of
      the night."

[3]But I responded,
"I have taken off my robe.
   Should I get dressed again?
I have washed my feet.
   Should I get them soiled?"

[4]My lover tried to unlatch the door,
   and my heart thrilled within me.
[5]I jumped up to open the door for
      my love,
   and my hands dripped with
      perfume.
My fingers dripped with lovely
      myrrh
   as I pulled back the bolt.
[6]I opened to my lover,
   but he was gone!
   My heart sank.
I searched for him
   but could not find him
      anywhere.
I called to him,
   but there was no reply.
[7]The night watchmen found me
   as they made their rounds.
They beat and bruised me
   and stripped off my veil,
   those watchmen on the walls.

[8]Make this promise, O women
      of Jerusalem—
   If you find my lover,
   tell him I am weak with love.

Young Women of Jerusalem

⁹Why is your lover better than
    all others,
    O woman of rare beauty?
What makes your lover so special
    that we must promise this?

Young Woman

¹⁰My lover is dark and dazzling,
    better than ten thousand others!
¹¹His head is finest gold,
    his hair is black as a raven.
¹²His eyes sparkle like doves
    beside springs of water;
they are set like jewels
    washed in milk.
¹³His cheeks are like gardens
        of spices
    giving off fragrance.
His lips are like lilies,
    perfumed with myrrh.
¹⁴His arms are like rounded bars
        of gold,
    set with beryl.
His body is like bright ivory,
    glowing with lapis lazuli.

¹⁵His legs are like marble pillars
    set in sockets of finest gold.
His posture is stately,
    like the noble cedars of Lebanon.
¹⁶His mouth is sweetness itself;
    he is desirable in every way.
Such, O women of Jerusalem,
    is my lover, my friend.

Young Women of Jerusalem

6 Where has your lover gone,
    O woman of rare beauty?
Which way did he turn
    so we can help you find him?

Young Woman

²My lover has gone down to his
        garden,
    to his spice beds,
to browse in the gardens
    and gather the lilies.
³I am my lover's, and my lover
        is mine.
    He browses among the lilies.

1. Why does the woman back off when the man invites her to intimacy (5:3)?

THE POETIC IMAGINATION

The Song of Songs is a poem that intends to evoke feelings and stimulate the imagination, not describe an actual relationship. If it's read as a realistic account, much of the action of this poem will seem preposterous. How could we explain the woman's virtual indifference about being beaten and stripped by watchmen if it really happened? More likely the watchmen are a poetic metaphor representing any forces hostile to intimacy; in the power of her desire, the woman moves past these obstacles to be with her beloved.

2. Why do you think the man has withdrawn after his initial attempt to be with the woman?

3. The poem describes the man moving toward the woman and the woman moving toward the man, but not at the same time. How is this an accurate poetic representation of difficulties couples can have connecting with each other?

4. How would you describe the woman's feelings when she opens the door?

What does she then do?

5. Once she decides to be with the man but finds him gone, what obstacles does she encounter as she tries to be with him?

What does her response to these obstacles tell us about the strength of her desire?

6. As she enlists her friends to help her find the man, she describes him to them. What do you learn about her feelings toward him from the description she gives (5:10-16)?

7. Does the poem end happily or unhappily (6:3)?

Is this true to life? Why or why not?

8. What commitments allow couples to overcome problems with intimacy?

▶ **FOR THE COUPLE**

Imagine yourselves as the woman and man in this text. What is going through their minds as the man moves toward the woman but she moves away?

as the woman moves toward the man but he moves away?

Does any of this ring true to your relationship?

How do the woman and man feel as they are reunited (6:2-3)?

Have you experienced this kind of joyful closeness after making your way through conflicts?

▶ BONUS

Read Song of Songs 2:10-15. After talking about the beauty of the garden as a place to share intimacy, the chorus of young women warns about the danger of the foxes destroying the vineyard. What do the foxes represent?

LEADER'S NOTES

My grace is sufficient for you.

2 CORINTHIANS 12:9 NIV

Leading a Bible discussion can be an enjoyable and rewarding experience. But it can also be *scary*—especially if you've never done it before. If this is your feeling, you're in good company. When God asked Moses to lead the Israelites out of Egypt, he replied, "O Lord, please send someone else to do it" (Ex 4:13 NIV). It was the same with Solomon, Jeremiah and Timothy, but God helped these people in spite of their weaknesses, and he will help you as well.

You don't need to be an expert on the Bible or a trained teacher to lead a Bible discussion. The idea behind these inductive studies is that the leader guides group members to discover for themselves what the Bible has to say. This method of learning will allow group members to remember much more of what is said than a lecture would.

These studies are designed to be led easily. As a matter of fact, the flow of questions through the passage from observation to interpretation to application is so natural that you may feel that the studies lead themselves. This study guide is also flexible. You can use it with a variety of groups—student, professional, neighborhood or church groups. Each study takes forty-five to sixty minutes in a group setting.

There are some important facts to know about group dynamics and encouraging discussion. The suggestions listed below should enable you to effectively and enjoyably fulfill your role as leader.

PREPARING FOR THE STUDY

1. Ask God to help you understand and apply the passage in your own life. Unless this happens, you will not be prepared to lead others. Pray too for the various members of the group. Ask God to open your hearts to the message of his Word and motivate you to action.

2. Read the introduction to the entire guide to get an overview of the entire book and the issues which will be explored.

3. As you begin each study, read and reread the assigned Bible passage to familiarize yourself with it.

4. This study guide is based on the New Living Translation of the Bible. It will help you and the group if you use this translation as the basis for your study and discussion.

5. Carefully work through each question in the study. Spend time in meditation and reflection as you consider how to respond.

6. Write your thoughts and responses in the space provided in the study guide. This will help you to express your understanding of the passage clearly.

7. It might help to have a Bible dictionary handy. Use it to look up any unfamiliar words, names or places. (For additional help on how to study a passage, see chapter five of *How to Lead a LifeGuide Bible Study*, InterVarsity Press.)

8. Consider how you can apply the Scripture to your life. Remember that the group will follow your lead in responding to the studies. They will not go any deeper than you do.

9. Once you have finished your own study of the passage, familiarize yourself with the leader's notes for the study you are leading. These are designed to help you in several ways. First, they tell you the purpose the study guide author had in mind when writing the study. Take time to think through how the study questions work together to accomplish that purpose. Second, the notes provide you with additional background information or suggestions on group dynamics for various questions. This informa-

tion can be useful when people have difficulty understanding or answering a question. Third, the leader's notes can alert you to potential problems you may encounter during the study.

10. If you wish to remind yourself of anything mentioned in the leader's notes, make a note to yourself below that question in the study.

LEADING THE STUDY

1. Begin the study on time. Open with prayer, asking God to help the group to understand and apply the passage.

2. Be sure that everyone in your group has a study guide. Encourage the group to prepare beforehand for each discussion by reading the introduction to the guide and by working through the questions in the study.

3. At the beginning of your first time together, explain that these studies are meant to be discussions, not lectures. Encourage the members of the group to participate. However, do not put pressure on those who may be hesitant to speak during the first few sessions. You may want to suggest the following guidelines to your group.

   • Stick to the topic being discussed.

   • Your responses should be based on the verses that are the focus of the discussion and not on outside authorities such as commentaries or speakers.

   • Anything said in the group is considered confidential and will not be discussed outside the group unless specific permission is given to do so.

   • Listen attentively to each other and provide time for each person present to talk.

   • Pray for each other.

4. Play the DVD clip from the *Intimate Marriage DVD* and use the DVD reflection question to kick off group discussion. You can move directly from there to the beginning of the study section. Or, if you wish, you can also have a group member read the introduction aloud and then you can discuss the question in the "Open" section. If you do not have the DVD, then

be sure to kick off the discussion with the question in the "Open" section.

The "Open" question and the DVD clip are meant to be used before the passage is read. They introduce the theme of the study and encourage members to begin to open up. Encourage as many members as possible to participate, and be ready to get the discussion going with your own response.

This section is designed to reveal where your thoughts or feelings need to be transformed by Scripture. That is why it is especially important not to read the passage before the discussion question is asked. The passage will tend to color the honest reactions people would otherwise give because they are, of course, supposed to think the way the Bible does.

5. Have a group member (or members if the passage is long) read aloud the passage to be studied. Then give people several minutes to read the passage again silently so that they can take it all in.

6. Question 1 will generally be an overview question designed to briefly survey the passage. Encourage the group to look at the whole passage, but try to avoid getting sidetracked by questions or issues that will be addressed later in the study.

7. As you ask the questions, keep in mind that they are designed to be used just as they are written. You may simply read them aloud. Or you may prefer to express them in your own words.

    There may be times when it is appropriate to deviate from the study guide. For example, a question may have already been answered. If so, move on to the next question. Or someone may raise an important question not covered in the guide. Take time to discuss it, but try to keep the group from going off on tangents.

8. The sidebars contain further background information on the texts in the study. If they are relevant to the course of your discussion, you may want to read them aloud. However, to keep the discussion moving, you may want to omit them and allow group members to read them on their own.

9. Avoid answering your own questions. If necessary, repeat or rephrase them until they are clearly understood. Or point out something you read in the

leader's notes to clarify the context or meaning. An eager group quickly becomes passive and silent if they think the leader will do most of the talking.

10. Don't be afraid of silence. People may need time to think about the question before formulating their answers.

11. Don't be content with just one answer. Ask, "What do the rest of you think?" or "Anything else?" until several people have given answers to the question.

12. Acknowledge all contributions. Try to be affirming whenever possible. Never reject an answer. If it is clearly off-base, ask, "Which verse led you to that conclusion?" or again, "What do the rest of you think?"

13. Don't expect every answer to be addressed to you, even though this will probably happen at first. As group members become more at ease, they will begin to truly interact with each other. This is one sign of healthy discussion.

14. Don't be afraid of controversy. It can be very stimulating. If you don't resolve an issue completely, don't be frustrated. Move on and keep it in mind for later. A subsequent study may solve the problem.

15. Periodically summarize what the group has said about the passage. This helps to draw together the various ideas mentioned and gives continuity to the study. But don't preach.

16. At the end of the Bible discussion, give couples an opportunity to discuss the "For the Couple" section and make the application personal. It's important to include this in your group time so that couples don't neglect discussing this material. Of course, sometimes couples may need to discuss the topic long beyond the five minutes of group time allotted, but you can help them get started in the meeting.

17. Encourage group members to work on the "Bonus" section between meetings as a couple or on their own. Give an opportunity during the session for people to talk about what they are learning.

18. End on time.

Many more suggestions and helps on leading a couples group are found in the *Intimate Marriage Leader's Guide*.

COMPONENTS OF SMALL GROUPS

A healthy small group should do more than study the Bible. There are four components to consider as you structure your time together.

Nurture. Small groups help us to grow in our knowledge and love of God. Bible study is the key to making this happen and is the foundation of your small group.

Community. Small groups are a great place to develop deep friendships with other Christians. Allow time for informal interaction before and after each study. Plan activities and games that will help you get to know each other. Spend time having fun together—going on a picnic or cooking dinner together.

Worship and prayer. Your study will be enhanced by spending time praising God together in prayer or song. Pray for each other's needs—and keep track of how God is answering prayer in your group. Ask God to help you to apply what you are learning in your study.

Outreach. Reaching out to others can be a practical way of applying what you are learning, and it will keep your group from becoming self-focused. Host a series of evangelistic discussions for your friends or neighbors. Clean up the yard of an elderly friend. Serve at a soup kitchen together, or spend a day working on a Habitat house.

Many more suggestions and helps in each of these areas are found in *Small Group Idea Book.* Information on building a small group can be found in *The Big Book on Small Groups* (both from InterVarsity Press). Reading through one of these books would be worth your time.

STUDY NOTES

Study 1. Desire and Ecstasy. Song of Songs 6:13—7:13.

Purpose: To discover how God regards desire between a married man and woman.

General note. An often-neglected biblical resource on sexual desire is the tiny book of poems known as the Song of Songs, a name indicating that this song is the most sublime of all songs. The content is so erotic that the Christian church has not always known what to do with it. During times when it was thought that sexuality was at odds with spirituality, the book was treated as an allegory, a figurative poem whose real theme was the relationship between God or Christ and the church.

However, a straightforward reading of the text reveals that it is a love poem, indeed a collection of love poems that celebrate romantic affection between human beings and sexual desire between a husband and a wife.

The poem that is the focus of this Bible study and the two poems of study two are a special kind of love poem within the collection of love poems that we know as the Song of Songs. Scholars call such a poem a *wasf*, an Arabic term that means "description." The Arabic term is used because scholars have noted a similarity with modern Arabic wedding poems. These poems describe the physical beauty of the groom or the bride from either the head down or the feet up. They are sensuous descriptions and are preludes to lovemaking. In modern parlance, these poems set the mood for romance.

Question 1. Notice in particular the level of desire expressed by the man's wanting to climb the palm tree and grasp its fruit (7:7-8). The palm tree with its fruit represents his beloved. Aroused with longing, he desires to be physically intimate with her, bringing his body up against hers. Her breasts, represented by the clusters of fruit, loom large in his imagination.

Notice also how he compares her kisses to wine, a sensuous liquid that makes a person lightheaded (7:9); the kisses of one's beloved have the same intoxicating effect. The image is of wine in the woman's mouth flowing into the mouth of the man, indicating intimacy of the most pleasurable kind.

Question 3. Throughout the Song of Songs, the countryside represents a place of seclusion and privacy, while city settings are full of people and are therefore not conducive to romantic meetings. This, of course, doesn't mean that lovers need to go to country settings; it does mean that intimate, romantic moments require privacy.

Questions 4 and 6. The imagery-rich language of the Song of Songs is anything but prudish. It is sensuous and erotic. It makes some readers of the

Bible uncomfortable. But the Song is the Word of God, and God knows that married couples need to hear this language in order to know just how important God thinks it is for them to be sexually intimate.

The Bible version used in these studies is the New Living Translation, an excellent one, being both readable and accurate. The translators have chosen to help the modern reader to understand the meaning of difficult metaphors by introducing descriptive words or phrases that are not in the Hebrew but are implied in the metaphor. For instance, Song of Songs 7:4 is translated "Your neck is as beautiful as an ivory tower." A literal translation of the Hebrew would be simply "Your neck is an ivory tower"; the term *beautiful* is added. Thus we should use the NLT's description as a start, but we may also allow our imagination to suggest other connections.

The meaning of any metaphor is difficult to express with a single word. Metaphors resonate deeply and richly and evoke emotions. We will not be able to capture all the sense of the metaphors, so don't be discouraged if your ideas are not found in the description below.

Legs like jewels: Jewels of course are precious. The rounded shape of her legs appeals to him. A skilled craftsman couldn't have made them any lovelier. The word translated "jewel" can also be understood as a "ring" and may refer to the curve of the woman's inner thigh.

Navel like a rounded goblet: An exposed navel is quite sensuous, particularly in ancient society where everyday clothes were not at all revealing. And the eroticism of this image is heightened if the "navel" actually represents the woman's vagina, as most biblical scholars suggest. Of course a navel (as well as a vagina) is gobletlike and could literally be filled with a liquid. He will drink from her navel. There is no vulgarity or shame in this allusion to oral sex.

Belly like a heap of wheat: One common understanding of this image is that it pictures a bundle of wheat bound in the middle, suggesting a slender waist. But more likely, according to biblical scholars, is that this is another reference to the woman's vagina, since the word translated "belly" can also refer to the woman's reproductive organs. The wheat would then allude to her pubic hair.

Breasts like two fawns: Here we are to envision the fawns from the rear, their rounded bottoms with short tails suggesting soft breasts with protruding nipples.

Neck like an ivory tower: Towers are majestic, stately, powerful. Probably no real tower was ever made out of ivory, but ivory suggests opulence and perhaps jewelry that she would wear around her neck.

Eyes like the pools of Heshbon: Of course the metaphor of the pool suggests moist rather than dry eyes. Heshbon was a real city which must have had notably beautiful pools.

Nose like the tower of Lebanon: Size is not the issue here; rather, like the ivory tower, the image suggests stateliness, majesty.

Head like Mount Carmel: Carmel was renowned for its beauty. It was a luxurious mountain with resplendent trees. Like Carmel among mountains, so is her head among others.

Hair like royal tapestry: Of course *royal* tapestry was the finest type.

Stature like a palm: In his eyes she is thin and tall; he goes on to speak of climbing, which is evocative of sexual intimacy.

Breasts like clusters of fruit: They attract his attention. He wants to fondle them. They emit a pleasant fragrance that attracts him, and he wants to taste their delicious juice.

Question 7. Shulammite means "contented" and indicates that the result of intimacy is a contented uniting of two people.

Bonus. It does seem paradoxical that in the same Bible in which Jesus' warnings about lust are found we have the Song of Songs, which uses many sensuous verbal images. But lust is not the same as desire. Lust is a desire to consume and control. It is natural and normal for an unmarried man or woman to desire intimacy with someone they love. The important thing is to be careful not to act on that desire until the marriage commitment is made.

Study 2. Different Bodies. Song of Songs 4:1—5:1, 10-16.

Purpose: To discuss the role of physical attraction in marriage.

Question 1. With sin's presence in the world, everyone feels less than adequate in every way, including physical attractiveness. Remember how Adam and Eve covered themselves from each other's gaze. We all feel as if we are not attractive enough.

That is one reason we need to hear encouraging words from others. Compliments between spouses invite openness and intimacy. It makes us feel safe to uncover ourselves in front of our spouse and join in intimate contact.

If someone cannot see the beauty in their spouse, the problem is theirs, not the spouse's. After all, everyone is created in the image of God and reflects his glory.

Question 2. The Song makes it clear that physical attraction to a person of the opposite sex is not wrong. Yet physical attraction should not be the whole reason or even the most important reason a couple comes together. Proverbs 31:30 does not say that beauty is totally worthless but that it is fleeting. What is important is the quality of a good relationship with the Lord; that survives the aging process. If one builds a relationship on good looks alone, it will not survive through the years of growing older. (See also the answer to the Bonus question.)

Question 3. The descriptive poems in the Song of Songs are quite sensuous and anything but prudish. They are honest expressions of desire; the man and the woman talk about their beloved's body in terms that are frank but not at all obscene or dirty. Depending on time, the couple or group will have to be selective here. Choose a few examples and spend time reflecting on what they might mean. Some of the images of the woman's beauty appeared in the passage studied in the previous session (see the note on questions 4 and 6); others are new.

The New Living Translation gives help by providing hints at what some of the more obscure images might mean. However, all English translations are sometimes overcautious about offending readers. A case in point is the NLT's rendition of 5:14: "His body is like bright ivory, glowing with lapis lazuli." This translation suggests a compliment on the man's complexion. A more straightforward translation is "His member is an ivory tusk, ornamented with lapis." Such an honest translation reminds married couples that it is healthy and appropriate to be drawn to the sexuality of one's spouse.

Question 4. As noted in the sidebar, the imagery of the garden in this section is a tasteful way of referring to the most private place on the woman's body. The man's description of her garden is rapturous. It is the ultimate focus of his attention. That she invites him into her garden points to her desire for physical intimacy with him. The man's words about gathering spices and eating and drinking sensual liquids communicate his joy in the union.

Question 5. All the senses are aroused in these poems. The physical descriptions of the man's and woman's beauty most clearly use the sense of sight, but there are also references to fragrance, touch, hearing and even taste. Love excites all the senses. The Song invites a married couple to let their senses deeply enjoy each other's body.

Question 6. By virtue of the fact that the language is found in Holy Scripture, we can say that it is definitely appropriate. But it is appropriate only when applied in the right situation. In this case, it is a man and a woman speaking privately to each other. Within the context of marriage commitment, such intimacies not only are allowed but also serve to build up a relationship.

Question 7. The caves and wild animals represent a place that is dangerous and away from his protection. He uses this language to encourage her to come into the comfort and protection of his embrace.

Bonus. The passage in Peter makes it clear that the most important type of beauty is inward. In a thought similar to Proverbs 31:30, physical beauty is second to a woman's faith and personality. However, to say spiritual beauty is more important does not mean that concern with one's physical beauty is totally irrelevant. And besides that, physical beauty is enhanced by spiritual beauty and a good personality. Beauty is in the eye of the beholder.

Study 3. Time for Passion. Song of Songs 1:2-4, 7-17.

Purpose: To learn how to make time to draw each other into sexual intimacy.

Question 1. She desires to touch and taste him with her kisses; she smells his fragrant cologne. She loves to hear his name. These sensual experiences arouse her desire to go with him to his bedroom for intimacy. In the same way, we may be aroused sexually through foreplay that involves all the senses.

Question 2. Wine is a liquid that leaves a strong and, to many people, pleasant aftertaste. Wine also produces a lightheadedness that is similar to the effect of kissing one's beloved. As a matter of fact, elsewhere the Song speaks of the *intoxicating* effect of love (5:1).

Question 3. If a woman loves, respects and honors a man, and a man loves, respects and honors a woman, it is much easier to be intimate as a couple.

Question 4. It is hard to understand this passage if you don't think it is appropriate for a woman to initiate intimacy. Some cultural stereotypes, especially among Christians, can discourage a woman from expressing her desire to be physically intimate with her husband, but there is nothing in the Bible to discourage the idea that both men and women can pursue relationship.

Question 5. Remember, the Song is a poem. The chorus doesn't represent any specific, concrete group of women. They serve a variety of purposes in the Song; here their function is to provide public affirmation of this relationship. They proclaim the union between the man and the woman a good thing.

Question 6. The poem is a kind of tease to build up sexual excitement. The woman's determination to be with her husband in spite of the obstacles shows her tremendous desire to be with him. And he teases her back. This provides an opportunity for him to describe a pastoral scene of goat trails and shepherd tents, which in the cultural context of these love songs is a romantic setting, particularly as opposed to the city.

Question 7. Some Christians think that jewels are ostentatious or even deceptive. But in the Song the woman's beauty is frequently described as enhanced by them. She often dresses seductively and wears fragrances that invite intimacy. The Bible condemns such attire when used to seduce someone outside of a marriage context (Prov 7:13-20) but celebrates it here within the commitment of marriage.

Beauty may not last, and relationships have to be built on something more lasting. However, we should not completely denigrate physical beauty as if it were not spiritual, and we should not use religion as an excuse not to take care of how we look. While it is wrong to arouse desire outside of marriage, it is appropriate to try to seduce our spouse.

Bonus. It is impossible to do this infallibly, but it begins by being attentive to oneself and one's spouse. It is important to realize moments that are conducive to intimacy and those things that work against it. One can cultivate those things (compliments, gifts, getting alone, helping) that lead to romance.

Study 4. Overcoming Contempt and Shame. Genesis 2:25—3:17; 2 Samuel 6:14-16, 20-22.

Purpose: To understand how the past affects our marriage and what we need to do to grow beyond it.

Question 1. Though it varies in degrees, human relationships are characterized by a struggle for power. Husbands and wives try to control their life by controlling their spouse. This may manifest itself in an aggressive wife or a quietly manipulative husband.

Question 2. Ultimately, each seeks to get his or her own way. However, sometimes a spouse may try to control the other in the belief that they are being helpful. They know the way to avoid trouble, so they insist that their spouse do what they say.

Question 3. Of course it hurts intimacy. The mutual desire to wrest control drives a husband and wife apart, not toward each other.

Question 4. As we will see in a future study, the solution will be to give up the illusion of gaining control and adopting a lifestyle of mutual submission, confession, forgiveness and reconciliation.

Question 5. Michal reacts with anger and disgust to her husband's ecstatic dance before the ark of the covenant. On the surface of it, we might think she was justified in being upset about her husband's prancing scantily clad around the ark in front of servant girls. However, the narrative sides with David. David is celebrating the Lord, and his lack of self-consciousness is positive.

It is Michal who reaps negative consequences from their fight (v. 23). The fact that she is described as "the daughter of Saul" (vv. 16, 20) rather than "David's wife" is a clear indication (based on how Hebrews told their stories) that the real tension arises because she represents the remnant of those who support Saul over and against David.

Question 6. David's response to Michal definitely heightens the tension. He essentially tells her that he is fine with her disdain and is comforted by the fact that the servant girls hold him in high honor.

David and Michal are an example of how couples shouldn't react to each other. They push each other away by their anger and contempt. They haven't left their past loyalties to weave a new one. Michal still clings to her loyalty to her father, Saul, and David refuses to abandon the admiration of other women.

It should be pointed out again that this text is not about marriage but rather theology and politics, and in this regard the narrative is with David, who properly expresses enthusiasm toward God, and against Michal as one who would be on the side of her father Saul's failed kingship.

Question 7. Rather than Michal rushing to attack and David rushing to defense, they should talk about the situation. David's actions need to be placed in their proper context. His dancing without abandon in public did not seek to arouse other women but to celebrate and rejoice in God. Michal should have rejoiced with her husband, and David should have helped her see why his actions were not shameful.

Question 8. These emotions just push them apart rather than together.

For the Couple. Remember, feelings of shame are often rooted deeply in our past experiences, and it is possible for them to be triggered by a statement or action that in itself is completely innocent. That is, my feelings of shame are not necessarily the fault of my spouse.

The symbolic honoring of each other will be most meaningful if it connects somehow to the original offense or misunderstanding. For example, if something a husband said triggered his wife's feelings of deep shame about not being beautiful enough, he could take time to choose flowers for her and explain how these blooms remind him of her special attractiveness.

Study 5. Restoring Broken Trust. Psalm 55.

Purpose: To discover how to overcome fear and anxiety when we are wounded in marriage.

Question 1. The psalmist feels verbally assaulted; he says that people attack him and want to make trouble for him (v. 3). He feels physically threatened by them (v. 9). But most of all, he feels betrayed.

Question 2. The terrible truth is that the psalmist has been betrayed by an intimate friend (vv. 12-14). We do not know the precise situation or the identity of the friend, but neither is important. After all, the psalm wasn't written to provide a historical memory but a prayer that future worshipers could use to express their own emotions before God.

Question 3. The psalmist responds with shock, fear and then anger. His anger leads him to beg God to destroy the one who betrayed him.

Question 4. Most people probably experience the same range of emotions that we see here. It is shocking to think that someone close to us would attack us. When something so unexpected happens, we are scared and may become quite angry. If a friend is close, we have probably been vulnerable with her or him, letting our weaknesses be seen, and these now are being used against us.

Question 5. Our trust has been compromised. We have felt comfortable with a close friend or our spouse, and now they have attacked us, perhaps at our point of greatest weakness.

Question 6. Fear causes us to withdraw. We want to be far away from the next attack. We want to remove ourselves from danger. This withdrawal does not have to be physical; it can be emotional and quite subtle.

Question 7. In the first place, it is important for each person to be aware of how their words and actions affect their partner. Sometimes we unconsciously create conditions that result in anxiety and withdrawal. There needs to be good communication between husband and wife, honest sharing about what induces worry or worse.

Question 8. The person who feels attacked and nervous about the relationship needs to bring it to their spouse's attention. Of course, if one is already questioning whether the relationship merits trust and if one is in fear of being hurt again, this is difficult, to say the least. In any situation, this psalm becomes a model for taking worries and fears to the Lord.

Bonus. When there is the potential for danger in a relationship, it is important to be afraid and take precautions. Samson should have feared Delilah; she successfully deceived him to his harm. In an abusive relationship, appropriate fear should lead the offended spouse to get help.

Study 6. Love's Failure and Redemption. Song of Songs 5:2—6:3.

Purpose: To understand how to maintain closeness and sexual intimacy over time.

General note. The Song of Songs is a very sensuous book, but it is not crude. It often uses double entendre (double meanings) to describe intimate acts. In the context of the use of the theme in other ancient Near Eastern writings, the man's request to "open the door" is an invitation to an intimate embrace. The man's wet hair, the woman's washed feet (feet are often euphemistic for genitalia in the Old Testament), the woman's dripping hands, the man putting his hand through the hole (often taken as a lock or latch) are all more provocative than they appear on the surface.

Question 1. She tells him that she has already prepared for bed by taking off her clothes and washing her feet (in the Old Testament "feet" is often a euphemism for genitalia). She is saying that she is not in the mood for intimacy.

Question 2. Since the woman did not respond to his initial overture for intimacy, he must have felt rejected and moved away from her.

Question 3. The couple that never has problems with sexual intimacy is probably nonexistent. This text should provide an opportunity for the group to at least name some issues that keep them from enjoying a vital sex life (exhaustion, children, grudges, unrealistic expectations). See studies four and five.

Question 4. After initial reluctance, she desires to be with him (indicated by her hands dripping with perfume, her fingers with liquid myrrh). But now aroused, she finds that he is gone. She is totally deflated, but rather than sulking she pursues him.

Question 5. Most notably she encounters the watchmen. These watchmen are likely suspicious of a woman out alone late at night. They then brutalize her. As noted in the sidebar, this poem is not to be taken literally; the watchmen represent any forces that would keep the man and the woman separate from one another. The fact that the woman works her way through them to ultimately get to her man shows the strength of her desire for him. Love overcomes even the most vicious threats.

Question 6. For the details, you can look back at study two. Here we see her strong attraction to him as well as her respect for him.

Question 7. The poem ends happily: she finds the man and they unite in the garden, the setting of intimacy throughout the book. Not all stories of conflict end so well, but the text intends to encourage people: though every marriage has its moments of disconnection, it is possible to work through the obstacles and enjoy moments of great joy together.

Question 8. This poem does not address that question except to suggest that it means staying involved and pursuing the other. *Forgiveness,* another study guide in the Intimate Marriage Series, explores the crucial role forgiveness plays in love's redemption.

Bonus. The vineyard is a place of intimacy, and the foxes represent a threat to that intimacy. The leader may want to follow up with a question about what kinds of things would provide such a threat.